THE BOY WHO CRIED

CASSANDRA GAISFORD

CONTENTS

Praise for The Boy Who Cried	vii
Foreword	xi
About the Transformational Super Kids Series	xv |//

Chapter 1	1
Chapter 2	3
Chapter 3	5
Chapter 4	7
Chapter 5	9
Chapter 6	11
Chapter 7	13
Chapter 8	15
Chapter 9	17
Chapter 10	19
Chapter 11	21
Chapter 12	23
Chapter 13	25
Chapter 14	27
Chapter 15	29
Chapter 16	31
Chapter 17	33
Chapter 18	35
Chapter 19	37
Chapter 20	39
Chapter 21	41
Chapter 22	43
Chapter 23	45

Chapter 24	47
Chapter 25	49
Chapter 26	51
Chapter 27	53
Chapter 28	55
Chapter 29	57
Chapter 30	59
Chapter 31	61
Chapter 32	63
Chapter 33	65
Chapter 34	67
Chapter 35	69
Chapter 36	71
Chapter 37	73
Chapter 38	75
Author's Note	77
Afterword	81
Free Workbook!	83
About the Author	85

EXCERPT: THE LITTLE PRINCESS

Praise for The Little Princess	89
Chapter 1	93
Chapter 2	95
Chapter 3	97
Chapter 4	99
Did you enjoy this excerpt?	101

EXCERPT: HOW TO FIND YOUR PASSION AND PURPOSE

Praise for How to Find Your Passion and Purpose — 105
Author's Note — 107
Introduction — 111
1. What Can Passion Do? — 123
2. The Power Of Passion — 125
3. Regret — 127
4. A Sense Of Caring Deeply — 129
5. Focus On Your Strengths — 131
Did you enjoy this excerpt? — 133

Also by Cassandra Gaisford — 135
Stay In Touch — 141
Copyright — 145

PRAISE FOR THE BOY WHO CRIED

"Being released from the trauma ...

This story is about the gaining of true power in growing into one's true self through childhood pain, discovering a new way of being, and knowing how where to go to gain help with being released from the trauma that had become one boys life. It is in the Author's Notes that this story transforms from a book to help children into a valuable resource for therapist and others who work with boys of all ages. Cassandra has captured a very typical aspect of how many boys are parented and the resulting chaos that becomes their adult-self. For those of us fortunate enough to have the privilege of working with men (boys of all ages) this sad yet beautiful story is one to keep handy and to share broadly.

> ~ **Catherine Sloan, Counsellor and Intuitive Therapist**

"Such a powerful message…

Sadly beautiful and a real reflection of our current society, which if we are really honest has lost direction, particularly with regards family values. Training in family values is an absolute pre-requisite before change will occur. I took pleasure in finding out the boy who cried not only survived but was blessed following the day the tears stopped and he found contentment, grace, and peace. My prayer is we can only attempt to save many more such boys."

> ~ **Kenn Butler, CEO**

"A wonderful tool…

This book is a wonderful tool for anyone seeking to begin the journey to self-reflection and healing from difficult childhoods. Therapists will find this book useful for their patients young or old. To return as a child to discover where the source of the pain begins has always been valuable, but actually relating it to present day is key to understanding. Highly recommended."

~ Alma Hammond, Author

FOREWORD

"Sadly a beautiful and a real reflection of our current society, which if we are really honest has lost direction, particularly with regards family values.

Training in traditional or cultural values pertaining to the family structure, function, roles, beliefs, attitudes, & ideals is an absolute pre-requisite before change will occur.

The author did not ask for my opinions on social issues, however my comments are intended to reflect how this story epitomises where our society has fallen today. The data in child abuse alone supports these views.

I took pleasure in finding out the boy who cried not only survived, but was blessed following the day the tears stopped and he found contentment, grace and peace.

My prayer is we can only attempt to save many more such boys."

~ Kenn Butler, CEO

DEDICATION

For the sensitive children

I have counselled

You inspire me

ABOUT THE TRANSFORMATIONAL SUPER KIDS SERIES

From the bestselling author of *The Little Princess* comes a brilliant new series, *Transformational Super Kids*.

These young heroes and heroines tackle modern-day problems with the passion and gusto of warriors.

They defeat cruel critics, they slay savage self-esteem demons, and they show people—jealous of their kindness, talent, and beauty—that their biggest superpower is staying true to themselves.

Suitable for 'kids' of all ages. After all, aren't we all still children at heart?

1

Once upon a time, there was a boy with the sensitivity of a butterfly and the strength of a samurai.

2

But no one valued his sensitivity.

So he covered it up.

When he grew older he became a warrior instead.

Hard. Fierce. Tough.

3

*a*t least that was the face he showed to the world.

But...
Inside, he cried.

4

𝒯o numb his pain he drank.

And drank.

And drank.

5

 ntil in a rage of anger, hurt, and despair he broke.

6

*A*nd he lay on the ground,

Like Humpty Dumpty who had a big fall.
And all the king's horses and all the king's men,
couldn't put the man together again.

7

ou've always hated us," his parents scolded when, as an adult, he tried to explain and heal his sorrow.

8

"That's not true. I love you.

I just want you to know how I felt as a child.

I want you to understand how I suffered.

I'm trying to figure out why I feel like I do.

I want to make peace with my past."

9

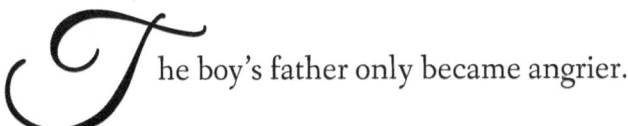
The boy's father only became angrier.

10

ou had a happy childhood," he growled.

11

"I was sad," his son tried to explain.

"I'm not trying to blame."

12

*H*is father listened, but he refused to hear.

His father refused to hear his son's story.

He refused to hear how his choice that the family become Jehovah's Witnesses had changed the little boys life.

13

*H*is father refused to hear how, as a six-year-old, being told he had to shun his cousins and uncles, and family and friends, had traumatised him.

His father refused to hear when the boy told him that he'd lived in fear the world was going to end.

But it never did.

14

𝓗is father refused to hear how moving to a foreign country and not being able to speak their language made him stressed and anxious.

And lonely.

15

His father refused to hear how as a little boy his son had always felt like an outsider.

16

The man's father listened but he refused to hear when he told him how being expelled for not singing the school's Christian anthem had made him distressed.

17

The boy's father refused to acknowledge that all the things that had happened to him when he was six. . . and seven. . . and eight. . . and nine made him anxious and gave him shingles when he was ten.

18

He tried to explain how unhappy he and his sister were as children, and how he'd suffered years later when she took her life.

At his sister's funeral his mother and father told him, "Good boy for not crying."

He tried to explain how it still hurt not to have a sister.

But his father didn't want want to talk about his son's feelings. Not then. And not now.

19

His father didn't care.

Instead of empathy, compassion, and tenderness, his father turned a deaf ear.

Instead of sadness, softness, and sorrow his father fortified his stony heart.

20

𝒜nd still the boy tried to show his father his love.

"I'm not telling you these things to hurt you," his son said.

"For fifty years I never told you. For fifty years I've kept my pain inside. For fifty years I slowly died."

21

"I want to let go of my hurt, my anger, and my sorrow," he said.

"I want to live what's left of my life like there's no tomorrow. I don't want to die with all these feelings and memories and ghosts trapped inside."

22

*A*nd then he stopped talking and waited.

Waited for his father to tell him he'd been heard. Waited for his father to tell him he cared. Waited for his father to tell him he was loved.

23

ut all he heard was silence.

24

He pressed the telephone to his ear.

"Dad? Are you still there?"

25

26

 ut all he heard was silence.

27

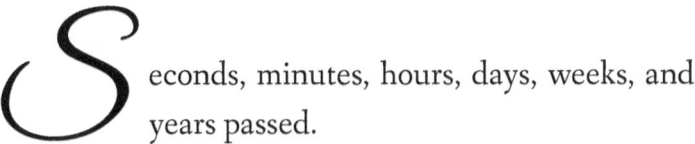

Seconds, minutes, hours, days, weeks, and years passed.

28

 ut all he heard was silence.

29

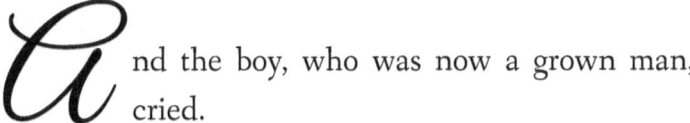

And the boy, who was now a grown man, cried.

30

He cried with relief as his painful feelings were released.

He cried with sorrow for the family he never had.

He cried with anguish for the reconciliation his father had shunned and refused and denied.

31

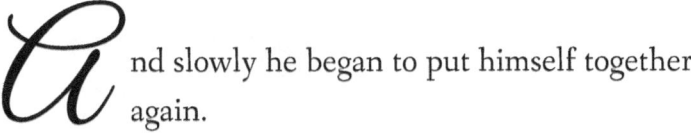

And slowly he began to put himself together again.

32

*H*e stopped looking for comfort in a bottle.

He stopped expecting his parents to change.

He stopped reaching out to them again, and again, and again.

33

He started putting energy into things that gave him joy.

He started devoting himself to people who really understood him—the adult and the boy.

He started becoming the hero of his past.

34

𝓐nd he began sharing his story...

In the little book you are reading now :)

35

*a*nd the big man cried.

He cried tears of joy when he was laughing with his friends.

He cried with excitement when he conquered impossible feats.

He cried with pride when he shared his passion with people all over the world.

36

He cried with purpose when he was able to help, and empathise and offer practical counsel to other men struggling to survive.

37

*A*nd he felt loved when people told him that he mattered, that he was kind, and they thanked him for making a difference to their lives.

38

Then one day the tears stopped.

And in the emptiness, his heart danced with acceptance, grace, and peace.

*** THE END ***

AUTHOR'S NOTE

I wrote this book in the notes section of my iPhone during a long flight from New Zealand to New York in 2019.

My first two books in The Transformational Super Kids series had been inspired by my own experience of being bullied, and also my daughter's. I thought, "what about the boys? They suffer too."

The words came in a flash of inspiration. I drew upon my experiences as a child therapist counselling children as young as six who had been traumatised.

Some had been abandoned by their parents. Others had been taken from their mom or dad (sometimes both) for their own protection. Then there were the children, who had been traumatised by their upbringing and the impact of their parents extreme beliefs.

Many of these kids were sent for 'anger management' by their schools or worried families.

Teenagers, young adults and men as mature as eighty also came for help with their anger. Some referred by the Courts, others by fed-up spouses.

I quickly discovered that, whatever their reasons for coming, below their anger was a deep well of sadness and despair. I say 'quickly' but in reality it took considerable skill, insight and compassion to gain their trust.

For, regardless of their age, these boys, had spent their lives, be it six-years, or 80, learning to hide their vulnerability. Almost all of them had grown up being told, "boys don't cry' in one variation or another.

I listened carefully to their stories. I kept my ears open to their sorrow and their pain. I held space when at last I heard their tears.

Tears tell truths, I told them. It's not weak to cry.

And soon, where once were warriors, beautiful, loving, caring boys reemerged.

And so did their dreams, their hopes, and their aspirations.

Like Jake, then eight-years-young, sent to me because he was so violent and aggressive at school and at home, who told me he wanted to be a policeman when he grew up so he could make the world a safer place.

I'll share his transformational story in another book in this series...coming soon.

THE BOY WHO *Cried* is now available as an audiobook for your listening enjoyment. Check out a free sample or grab your copy from your library or favourite online retailer.

AFTERWORD

In *Emptiness Dancing*, Adyashanti, an American spiritual teacher and author, encourages us to wake up to the essence of who and what we are, through the natural and spontaneous opening of our mind, heart, and body.

Life offers many opportunities for spontaneous healing. Sometimes we proactively invite it, other times we must confront the sources of our pain, wounds, and sorrow. It is only when we have the courage to listen and voice and release our traumatic pasts that we discover the secret to happiness and liberation.

Afterword

I hope you have found comfort, and healing from *The Boy Who Cried*. You may enjoy listening to the audiobook version, narrated by me. Available now.

Read to the end for an excerpt from the first book in this series—my #1 bestselling book, *The Little Princess*. It's inspired by my own story of being criticised, bullied and shamed and how I found the courage to follow my purpose.

As a special thank you for reading my book I have also included an excerpt from my popular book *How to Find Your Passion and Purpose*. I've included some of my favourite chapters. Please note these aren't in the order that they appear in the book.

To learn more about the inspiration behind this book and the series please visit my blog. You may also enjoy my regular inspirational newsletters—with sneak peeks, advance reads and free giveaways.

Be the first to know when other books in the Transformational Super Kids series are released!

You'll find details in the Stay in Touch section to follow.

FREE WORKBOOK!

The Passion Journal: The Effortless Path to Manifesting Your Love, Life, and Career Goals

Thank you for your interest in my new book. To show my appreciation, I'm excited to be giving you another book for FREE!

Download the free *Passion Journal Workbook* here>>https://dl.bookfunnel.com/aepj97k2n1

I hope you enjoy it—it's dedicated to helping you live and work with passion, resilience and joy.

You'll also be subscribed to my newsletter and receive free giveaways, insights into my writing life, new release advance alerts and inspirational tips to help you live and work with passion, joy, and prosperity. Opt out at anytime.

ABOUT THE AUTHOR

CASSANDRA GAISFORD is best known as *The Queen of Uplifting Inspiration.*

A former holistic therapist, award-winning artist, and #1 bestselling author. A corporate escapee, she now lives and works from her idyllic lifestyle property overlooking the Bay of Islands in New Zealand.

Cassandra's unique blend of business experience and qualifications (BCA, Dip Psych.), creative skills, and wellness and holistic training (Dip Counselling, Reiki Master Teacher) blends pragmatism and commercial savvy with rare and unique insight and out-of-the-box-thinking for anyone wanting to achieve an extraordinary life.

EXCERPT: THE LITTLE PRINCESS

PRAISE FOR THE LITTLE PRINCESS

"A Little Book with a Powerful Message...
An important reminder to always be true to yourself and summon the courage to follow your passions... Only *you* can live your life...GO live it!"

~ Harley

"The Little Princess is my hero...

I am a Midlife Coach, which means I help women find their moxie to do what they might not have done in the first half of their lives...I think *The Little Princess* needs to be a "required reading" text book for us all...she cuts to the heart of the lesson all of us need to hear, over and over again. *The Little Princess* embodies courage. She is my hero."

~ Sheree Clark, Midlife Courage Coach

***"The Little Princess* is 'brilliant...**
Short concise & full of tremendous vision & wisdom, expressed lovingly. Many of the comments read true for my own journey. I recognize my passion to be different than many others, my persistence to succeed, & the pure joy I have at the end of each day when I lay down my head & give thanks."

~ Kenn Butler, CEO

"Very uplifting and inspiring...
I love everything Cassandra writes, the queen of uplifting inspiration! This is a little book, the story basically teaches you to have faith in your dreams, stand firm and don't let others rain on your parade.. We are all searching for purpose and passion, everybody hurts and sometimes we find ourselves on the receiving end of somebody else's insecurities, when they project their anger, jealousy etc onto us..

The old woman who puts the little princess down is really just jealous and stuck in her own life."

~ Reviewer UK

"A reminder of the truth in all of us…
The Little Princess is a great short story as a reminder of the truth in all of us; Don't judge, take loving kindness as a guideline in life, but stay true to yourself; A powerful message! Like all the books by this author, it is a guideline to live a wise life."

~ Maartje Jager, Designer

1

Once upon a time there was a young woman who wanted to make a difference in the world.

She wanted to help others. She wanted to help people overcome depression, anxiety, and feeling sad.

She wanted to to help them feel inspired, joyful and happy.

She just wasn't sure how.

2

One day she had an inspired idea. "I can help people find their passion and purpose," she thought.

Her heart fluttered then soared higher and higher and higher—far, far, far away.

Almost beyond the reach of her doubts and fears.

3

She felt so excited—but also scared. She decided to feel the fear and create something anyway.

She knew people often struggled to find the time to read, and she wanted to make it easy and fun for people to find inspiration and help.

She decided to design a pack of inspirational cards that would enable people to help themselves and become empowered to transform their lives.

The cards would give people ideas, encourage them to dream, and give them hope.

4

She thought about the angel cards that had given her so much relief when she was an anxious child.

"Wouldn't it be fun to create something similar?" she thought.

Each card would have an inspirational quote on one side and a self-help strategy on the other.

DID YOU ENJOY THIS EXCERPT?

Follow your heart! Heed the call for courage.

Feeling stuck, depressed or demotivated? There are so many reasons why you should follow your dreams. If you need some motivation, look no further than this book.

Part moral allegory and part spiritual autobiography, *The Little Princess* is a timeless charm which tells the story of a young woman who leaves the safety of fitting in with everyone else, to follow her heart.

Be inspired by this journey to transformation and self-acceptance, and self-belief as she learns to overcome the vagaries of adult behaviour. Her personal odyssey culminates in a voyage of self-belief, passion, and purpose.

From the best-selling author of Mid-Life Career Rescue, Stress Less and How to Find Your Passion and Purpose: a powerful, inspiring, and practical book about boosting resilience, overcoming obstacles and moving forward after life's inevitable setbacks.

Find out what strategies are sabotaging your success. Find and follow your passion and purpose faster.

Bonus: Free Excerpt from How to Find Your Passion and Purpose—overcome common obstacles to success easily (including the fear of failure, fear of success, fear of criticism—and others)

Available in eBook, paperback, hardback and audiobook from all great online retailers.

EXCERPT: HOW TO FIND YOUR PASSION AND PURPOSE

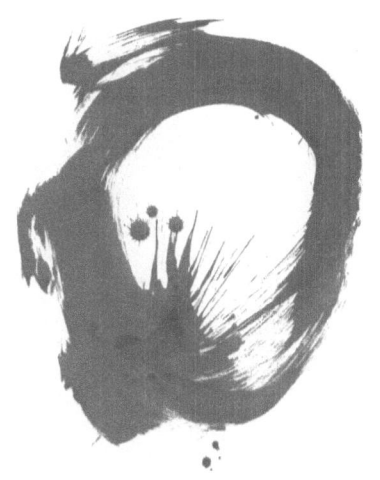

**PRAISE FOR HOW TO FIND YOUR
PASSION AND PURPOSE**

"This little book on a BIG topic that resonates with me packs a lot of wisdom that is worth investing time in. Cassandra challenges us to "Dare to Dream!" Take the time and make the effort to find the work you feel passionate about; You could read this in less than two hours and be on your way to sculpting out a new way of living if you're not living your passionate lifestyle yet."

~ Scott.B. Allan, Author of #1 bestseller *Empower Your Thoughts*

"This excellent little book is quick to read but left me with much to think about and many practical steps to take to find my passion and incorporate it into my life. There are several free resources to download which increase the worth of this already very valuable book."

~ Jenny Cliff, Author of *The Music Inside*

"*How to Find Your Passion and Purpose* is a positive and enabling companion and offers much. It encourages us to identify our passion and interests, to live from our core values and use our signature strengths creatively. It highlights that it's never too late to make changes, to get on the path of true fulfilment and make a living. Dig into this book and let Cassandra be your guide, inspiration and coach as she calls forth your creativity and gives practical steps to take you where you need to go next. Step into this ride joyfully and create your future."

~ Jasbindar Singh, Business Psychologist and Author of *Get Your Groove Back*

AUTHOR'S NOTE

This book is a concise guide to making the most of your life. It began its journey some years ago as *The Passion Pack* – a set of 40 cards created to help people live and work with passion.

The vision was simple: a few short, easy to digest tips for time-challenged people who were looking for inspiration and practical strategies to encourage positive change.

From my own experience, I knew that people didn't need a large wad of words to feel inspired, gain clarity and be stimulated to take action.

In coaching and counselling sessions I'd encourage my clients to ask a question they would like answered. The questions could be specific, such as, 'How can I make a living from my passion?' Or vague, for example, 'What do I most need to know?'

Then I'd ask them to pick a card at random. Without fail, they were astounded by the card's potent relevance. Disbelieving eyes widened in astonishment as they read either the quote or the main message they received. Many would say, "These cards are magic."

Orders flooded in from global recruitment consultancies, primary schools, colleges, universities, not-for-profit organisations, financial institutions and other multi-national commercial entities. I was asked to speak at conferences around the world about the power of passion. It was amazing to see how popular and successful *The Passion Pack* became, transcending age, gender, and socio-economic differences.

In this era of information obesity the need for simple, life-affirming messages is even more important. If you are looking for inspiration and practical tips, in short, sweet sound bites, this guide is for you.

Similarly, if you are a grazer, or someone more methodical, this guide will also work for you. Pick a page at random, or work through the steps sequentially. I encourage you to experiment, be open-minded and try new things. I promise you will achieve outstanding results.

Clive, a 62-year-old man who had suffered work-related burnout, did! He thought that creating a passion journal, *Tip 10* in this guide, was childish – something other stressed executives in his men's support group would balk at. But once he'd taken up the challenge he told me enthusiastically,

"They loved it!" They are using their passion journals to visualise, gain clarity, and create their preferred futures. Clive is using it to help manifest his new purpose-driven coaching business.

Let experience be your guide. Give your brain a well-needed break. Let go of 'why', and embrace how you *feel*, or how you want to feel. Honour the messages from your intuition and follow your path with heart.

Laura, who at one stage seemed rudderless career-wise, did just that. She was guided to *Tip 14: Who Inspires You?* Following that, her motivation to live and work like those she looked up to sparked a determination to start her own business. It was that simple.

At the time of writing I've just turned to Tip 31: *Fear Of Success*. It's a timely reminder of just how far following my passion has taken me – the shy girl who was once afraid of being seen. The quote is as apt for me as I feel it may be for you:

"Your playing small doesn't serve the world."

Here's to living with passion and purpose!

INTRODUCTION

"Mary Oliver says in one of her poems, 'Tell me, what is it that you plan to do with your one wild and precious life?' Me, I intend to live passionately."

Isabel Allende, Novelist

Finding a job you want and living a life you love is impossible without passion, enthusiasm, zest, inspiration and the deep satisfaction that comes from doing something that delivers you some kind of buzz.

Yet, it's staggeringly, and dishearteningly, true that many people don't know what they are passionate about, or how they can turn it into a rewarding career. Some research suggests that only 10% of people are living and working with passion. Hence my passion for passion and helping create more positive change in the world.

If you're like many people who don't know what they are passionate about or what gives your life meaning and purpose, this book will help provide the answers.

If you have been told it's not realistic to work and live with passion, this book will help change your mindset.

Together we'll help you get your mojo back, challenge your current beliefs and increase your sense of possibility. By tapping into a combination of practical career strategies, Law of Attraction principles, and the spiritual powers of manifestation, you'll reawaken dreams, boost your self-awareness, empower your life and challenge what you thought was possible.

We'll do this in an inspired yet structured way by strengthening your creative thinking skills, boosting your self-awareness and helping you identify your non-negotiable ingredients for career success and happiness. Little steps will lead naturally to bigger leaps, giving you the courage and confidence to follow your passion and fly free towards career happiness and life fulfilment.

What you're about to read isn't another self-help book; it's a self-empowerment book. It offers ways to increase your self-knowledge. From that knowledge comes the power to create a life worth living.

How to Find Your Passion and Purpose will help you:

- Explore and clarify your passions, interests, and life purpose
- Build a strong foundation for happiness and success
- Value your gifts, and talents and confirm your work-related strengths
- Direct your energies positively toward your preferred future
- Strengthen your creative thinking skills, and ability to identify possible roles you would enjoy, including self-employment
- Have the courage to follow your dreams and super-charge the confidence needed to make an inspired change
- Find your point of brilliance

Let's look briefly at what each chapter in this book will cover:

Step One, "The Call For Passion" will help you explore the meaning of passion and discover the benefits of following it, and consequences of ignoring your passion. You'll identify any passion blocking beliefs and intensify passion-building beliefs to boost your chances of success.

Step Two, "Discover Your Passion," will help you to identify your own sources of passion and passion criteria. What you'll discover may be a complete surprise and open up a realm of opportunities you've never considered.

Step Three, "Passion at Work," will assist you in identifying career options and exploring ways to develop your career in light of your passions and life purpose.

Step Four, "Live Your Passion," looks at passion beyond the world of work and ways to achieve greater balance and fulfilment. You'll also identify strategies to overcome obstacles and to maximise your success.

How to Find Your Passion and Purpose concludes with showing you how to identify your point of brilliance.

How To Use This Book—Your Virtual Coach

To really benefit from this book think of it as your 'virtual' coach—answer the questions and complete the additional exercises that you'll find in the chapters and free extras.

Questions are great thought provokers. Your answers to these questions will help you gently challenge current assumptions and gain greater clarity about your goals and desires.

All the strategies are designed to facilitate greater insight and to help you integrate new learnings. Resist the urge to just process information in your head. We learn best by doing. Research has repeatedly proven that the act of writing deepens your knowledge and understanding.

For example, a study conducted by Dr. David K. Pugalee, found that journal writing was an effective instructional tool and aided learning. His research found that writing helped people organise and describe internal thoughts and thus improve their problem solving-skills.

Henriette Klauser, Ph.D., also provides compelling evidence in her book, *Write It Down and Make It Happen*, that writing helps you clarify what you want and enables you to make it happen.

Writing down your insights is the area where people like motivational guru Tony Robbins, say that the winners part from the losers, because the losers always find a reason not to write things down. Harsh but perhaps true!

Keeping A Passion Journal

A passion journal is also a great place to store sources of inspiration to support you through the career planning and change process. For some tips to help you create your own inspirational passion journal, go to the media page on my website and watch my television interview and interview with other experts here:

http://www.cassandragaisford.com/media

This Book Is Magical

This book proves less really is more. Sometimes all it takes to radically transform your life is one word, one sentence, one powerful but simple strategy to ignite inspiration and reawaken a sense of possibility.

I have successfully used the knowledge I'm sharing with you in this book professionally with my clients and personally during numerous reinventions.

I stand by every one of the 4 steps and the 40+ strategies you will learn here, not just because they are grounded in strong evidence-based, scientific and spiritual principles, but also because I have successfully used them to create turnaround, after turnaround in nearly every area of my life.

How to Find Your Passion and Purpose is the culmination of all that I have experienced and all that I have learned, applied and taught others for over two decades. I don't practice what I preach; I preach what I have practiced—because it gets results.

Why Did I Write This Book?

If you are curious about *The Passion Pack* and why I created *How To Find Your Passion and Purpose*, you may like to check out my blog post here:

http://www.cassandragaisford.com/2557-2/

Setting You Up For Success

"Aren't you setting people up for failure?" a disillusioned career coach once challenged me.

Twenty-five years of cumulative professional experience as a career coach and counsellor, helping people work with passion and still pay the bills, answers that question. I'm setting people up for success. I'm not saying it will happen instantly, but if you follow the advice in this book, it will happen. I promise.

I've proven repeatedly, both personally and professionally, that thinking differently and creatively, rationally and practically, while also harnessing the power of your heart, and applying the principles of manifestation, really works. In this book, I'll show you why—and how.

A large part of my philosophy and the reason behind my success with clients is my fervent belief that to achieve anything worthy of life you need to follow your passion. And I'm in good company.

As media giant Oprah Winfrey once said, "Passion is energy. Feel the power that comes from focusing on what excites you."

Passion's Pay Cheque

By discovering your passion and purpose you will tap into a huge source of potential energy and prosperity. Pursuing your passion can be profitable on many levels:

- When you do what you love, your true talent will reveal itself; passion can't be faked
- You'll be more enthusiastic about your pursuits
- You'll have more energy to overcome obstacles
- You will be more determined to make things happen
- You will enjoy your work
- Your work will become a vehicle for self-expression
- Passion will give you a competitive edge

- You'll enjoy your life and magnetise positive experiences toward you

Without passion, you don't have energy, and without energy you have nothing.

You have to let love, desire, and passion, not fear or ambivalence or apathy, propel you forward. Yet worryingly, research suggests that less than 10% of people are following their passion. Perhaps that's why there is so much unhappiness in the world.

Don't waste another day feeling uninspired. Don't be the person who spends a life of regret, or waits until they retire before they follow their passions, be you. Don't be the person too afraid to make a change for the better, or who wishes they could lead a significant life. Make the change now. Before it's too late.

Extra Support: Companion Workbook

How to Find Your Passion and Purpose (the book) offers you information about overcoming adversity, building resilience and finding joy. Reading a book is great but applying the teachings and writing things down in a dedicated space helps bring the learning alive, deepens your self awareness, and enables you to make real world change. Reading gives you knowledge, but reflecting upon and applying that knowledge creates true empowerment.

By writing and recording your responses you're rewriting the story of your life. As Seth Godin states, "Here's the thing: The book that will most change your life is the book you write. The act of writing things down, of justifying your actions, of being cogent and clear, and forthright—that's how you change."

The *How to Find Your Passion and Purpose Companion Workbook* will support you through the learning and show you how to create real and meaningful change in your life...simply and joyfully.

Reach For Your Dreams

Passion, happiness, joy, fulfilment, love—call it what you will, my deepest desire is that this book encourages you to reach for your dreams, to never settle, to believe in the highest aspirations you have for yourself.

You have so many gifts, so many talents that the world so desperately needs. We need people like you who care about what they do, who want to live and work with passion and purpose.

I promise that if you follow the steps in this book you'll discover what you really want to do, clarify what you can do, and create powerful but simple strategies to make your dream a reality. You'll find a job that you love, one that adds more joy to your life and gives you a sense of meaning, purpose, and fulfilment.

And what I can promise you is this—whatever your circumstances, it's never too late to re-create yourself and your life. So, what are you waiting for?

Let's get started!

1
WHAT CAN PASSION DO?

**"Without passion, man is a mere latent force
and possibility, like the flint which awaits
the shock
of the iron before it can give forth its
spark."**
Henri-Frederic Amiel, Writer

Passion helps people lead bigger lives.
Passion is an indispensable part of success.
Passion helps people achieve.
Passion energises people.

Passion liberates people. It lets them be themselves.
Passion opens up fresh horizons.
Passion is good for your health and helps you live longer.

What will passion do for you?

2
THE POWER OF PASSION

"Passion is the fire that drives us to express
who we really are. Never deny passion,
for that is to deny who you are
and who you truly want to be."
Neale Walsch, Author

When people are pursuing something they are passionate about their energy, drive and determination is infinite. They become like pieces of elastic able to stretch to anything and accommodate any setback.

People immobilised by fear and passivity snap like a twig. They lack resilience.

Passion gives people a reason for living and the confidence, and drive to pursue their dreams.

RECORD all the reasons why you want more passion in your life. What are all the benefits that will flow?

** FREE BONUS **

If you haven't downloaded the free copy of the Passion Workbook, download it here—https://dl.bookfunnel.com/aepj97k2n1

3
REGRET

**"The worst thing one can do is be aware
of what one wants and not pursue it,
to spend years regretting things
never achieved or experiences never had."**
Jim Rohn, Writer

*S*ome people, who in their hearts know that they are capable of much more, never pursue their heart's desire. Regret because of a life not fully lived is a major source of depression, stress, and anger for many people.

You only get one shot at life. Don't spend it regretting opportunities you never took and dreams you never lived.

WHAT WOULD you do if you were 10 times bolder?

4
A SENSE OF CARING DEEPLY

"To succeed you have to believe in something with such a passion that it becomes a reality."
Anita Roddick, Businesswoman

Real passion is more than a fad or fleeting enthusiasm. It can't be turned on and off like a tap. It's a full-bodied belief or commitment to something.

. . .

What do you care deeply about? Discovering all the things that you feel strongly about is not always easy. Look for some clues to your beliefs by catching the times you use words such as "should" or "must."

What do you really believe in? It might be honesty, openness, freedom, equality, or justice. Record your insights in your passion journal.

5
FOCUS ON YOUR STRENGTHS

"Where talent and interest intersect expect a masterpiece."
John Ruskin, Painter

We often take our 'natural knacks' or gifts for granted. However, the skills that are easiest for us can provide a good clue to areas we are most passionate about. Sometimes others have a greater awareness of our strengths and areas of passion than we do!

What skills and talents come most naturally to you?

What strengths do others notice and admire?
What are the other skills and strengths that give you a buzz?

Write these insights in your passion journal. Add to it and review it regularly.

Passion flows, it can't be forced. Don't underestimate the things that come easiest for you.

DID YOU ENJOY THIS EXCERPT?

If you need more help to find and live your life purpose you can read my book, *How to Find Your Passion and Purpose: Four Easy Steps to Discover a Job You Want and Live the Life You Love* will help—available as a paperback and eBook and audiobook from all good online bookstores. I'm so excited to let you know that it will soon be available as an audio book—narrated by me!

Or you may prefer to take my online course, and watch inspirational and practical videos and other strategies to help you to fulfil your potential—https://the-coaching-lab.teachable.com/p/follow-your-passion-and-purpose-to-prosperity.

If you need more help to create a passion and purpose inspired business, *The Passion-Driven Business Planning Journal:The Effortless Path to Manifesting Your Business and Career Goals*, available as a paperback and eBook will help. Available from all good online bookstores.

ALSO BY CASSANDRA GAISFORD

Transformational Super Kids:

The Little Princess
I Have to Grow
The Little Boy Who Cried
The Little Princess Can Fly
Lulu is a Black Sheep
Jojo Lost Her Confidence
Why Doesn't Mummy Love Me?

Mid-Life Career Rescue:

The Call for Change
What Makes You Happy
Employ Yourself

Job Search Strategies That Work
3 Book Box Set: The Call for Change, What Makes You Happy, Employ Yourself
4 Book Box Set: The Call for Change, What Makes You Happy, Employ Yourself, Job Search Strategies That Work

Career Change:

Career Change 2020 5 Book-Bundle Box Set

Master Life Coach:

Leonardo da Vinci: Life Coach
Coco Chanel: Life Coach

The Art of Living:

How to Find Your Passion and Purpose
How to Find Your Passion and Purpose Companion Workbook
Career Rescue: The Art and Science of Reinventing Your Career and Life
Boost Your Self-Esteem and Confidence
Anxiety Rescue

Also by Cassandra Gaisford

No! Why 'No' is the New 'Yes'
How to Find Your Joy and Purpose
How to Find Your Joy and Purpose Companion Workbook

The Art of Success:

Leonardo da Vinci
Coco Chanel

Journaling Prompts Series:

The Passion Journal
The Passion-Driven Business Planning Journal
How to Find Your Passion and Purpose 2 Book-Bundle Box Set

Health & Happiness:

The Happy, Healthy Artist
Stress Less. Love Life More
Bounce: Overcoming Adversity, Building Resilience and Finding Joy
Bounce Companion Workbook

Mindful Sobriety:

Mind Your Drink: The Surprising Joy of Sobriety
Mind Over Mojitos: How Moderating Your Drinking Can Change Your Life: Easy Recipes for Happier Hours & a Joy-Filled Life
Your Beautiful Brain: Control Alcohol and Love Life More

Happy Sobriety:

Happy Sobriety: Non-Alcoholic Guilt-Free Drinks You'll Love
The Sobriety Journal
Happy Sobriety Two Book Bundle-Box Set: Alcohol and Guilt-Free Drinks You'll Love & The Sobriety Journal

Money Manifestation:

Financial Rescue: The Total Money Makeover: Create Wealth, Reduce Debt & Gain Freedom

The Prosperous Author:

Developing a Millionaire Mindset
Productivity Hacks: Do Less & Make More
Two Book Bundle-Box Set (Books 1-2)

Miracle Mindset:

Change Your Mindset: Millionaire Mindset Makeover: The Power of Purpose, Passion, & Perseverance

Non-Fiction:

Where is Salvator Mundi?

More of Cassandra's practical and inspiring workbooks on a range of career and life-enhancing topics are on her website (www.cassandragaisford.com) and her author page at all good online bookstores.

STAY IN TOUCH
FOLLOW ME AND CONTINUE TO BE INSPIRED

Become a fan and Continue To Be Supported, Encouraged, and Inspired

www.cassandragaisford.com
www.facebook.com/powerfulcreativity
www.instagram.com/cassandragaisford
www.youtube.com/cassandragaisfordnz
www.pinterest.com/cassandraNZ
www.linkedin.com/in/cassandragaisford
www.twitter.com/cassandraNZ

BLOG

Subscribe and be inspired by regular posts to help

you increase your wellness, follow your bliss, slay self-doubt, and sustain healthy habits.

Learn more about how to achieve happiness and success at work and life by visiting my blog:

www.cassandragaisford.com/archives

SPEAKING EVENTS

Cassandra is available internationally for speaking events aimed at wellness strategies, motivation, inspiration and as a keynote speaker.

She has an enthusiastic, humorous and passionate style of delivery and is celebrated for her ability to motivate, inspire and enlighten.

For information navigate to www.cassandragaisford.com/contact/speaking

To ask Cassandra to come and speak at your workplace or conference, contact: cassandra@cassandragaisford.com

NEWSLETTERS

For inspiring tools and helpful tips subscribe to Cassandra's free newsletters here:
http://www.cassandragaisford.com

Sign up now and receive a free eBook to help you find your passion and purpose!

COUNSELLING & WELLNESS THERAPIES

Navigate to the following page to learn more about my wellness therapies and coaching services and how they can help you:

http://www.cassandragaisford.com/wellness-therapies/

COPYRIGHT

Copyright © 2019, 2020 Cassandra Gaisford
Published by Blue Giraffe Publishing 2019

Blue Giraffe Publishing is a division of Worklife Solutions Ltd.

Cover Design by Steven Novak

All rights reserved. No part of this publication may be reproduced, distributed, or transmitted in any form or by any means, including photocopying, recording, or other electronic or mechanical methods, without the prior written permission of the author or publisher, except in the case of brief quotations embodied in reviews and certain other non-commercial uses permitted by copyright law.

Neither the publisher nor the author are engaged in rendering professional advice or services to the individual reader. The ideas, procedures, and suggestions contained in this book are not intended as a substitute for psychotherapy, counselling, or consulting with your physician.

The intent of the author is only to offer information of a general nature to help you in your quest for emotional, physical, and spiritual well-being.

Any use of information in this book is at the reader's discretion and risk. Neither the author nor the publisher can be held responsible for any loss, claim or damage arising out of the use, or misuse, of the suggestions made, the failure to take medical advice or for any material on third party websites.

ISBN PRINT: 978-0-9951250-7-0

ISBN EBOOK: 978-0-9951250-6-3

ISBN HARDCOVER: 978-0-9951288-2-8

Second Edition

www.ingramcontent.com/pod-product-compliance
Lightning Source LLC
Chambersburg PA
CBHW030438010526
44118CB00011B/698